UNDERSTANDING
PRACTICE ACCOUNTS

UNDERSTANDING
PRACTICE ACCOUNTS

Jenny Stone
Medical Accountant
Ramsay Brown and Partners, London

&

Ese Stacey
Director, mrcgpexam, Seaford

.:!MedicalPartnersPublishing

© **Medical Partners Publishing, 2007**

First published 2007

A CIP catalogue record for this book is available from the British Library.

ISBN 10: 0 9553661 0 0
ISBN 13: 978 0 9553661 0 9

Medical Partners Publishing
PO Box 2103, Seaford, East Sussex, BN25 1YZ
www.mrcgpexam.co.uk

Important Note from the Publisher

Typeset by Phoenix Photosetting, Chatham, Kent, UK
Printed by 4Edge Ltd, Hockley, Essex, UK

Contents

Preface

General practice is a business. Understanding the financial management of general practice is essential for the modern GP. Questions on practice accounts appear as part of the MRCGP exam and so GP registrars must understand them. However, it is clear that there is a real lack of knowledge in this area for both GP registrars and GP principals.

Understanding Practice Accounts explains practice accounts in a straight-forward, jargon-free way and includes detailed examples throughout to aid understanding.

Jenny Stone and Ese Stacey
July 2006

Abbreviations

ACA	Association of Chartered Accountants
CPI	Contractor Population Index
FCA	Fellow Chartered Accountant
FYA	first year allowance
GMS	General Medical Services
GSE	global sum equivalent
MIPG	Minimum Income Protection Guarantee
NI	national insurance
PCO	Primary Care Organization
PMS	Personal Medical Services
PSR	profit sharing ratios
QOF	quality and outcomes framework
SFE	Statement of Financial Entitlement

Chapter 1

Introduction to practice accounts

What are practice accounts?

Practice accounts are an historic record of the financial performance of the practice. The accounts themselves typically comprise two pages:
- the profit and loss account
- the balance sheet

The profit and loss account provides the practice with a record of all their income and expenses for a given period. It also provides the GPs of the practice with information about how much profit they have earned in any given period.

The balance sheet is rather like a snapshot and provides the practice with a record of the value of their assets and liabilities (liabilities are defined later, see page 11) at a given point in time. It also shows each GP their share of those assets.

All other pages and information in the accounts provide further explanation of the profit and loss account and the balance sheet.

Why do we need accounts?

To many GPs, the main purpose of accounts is to calculate the profits to be declared on their tax return which is submitted to the Inland Revenue. However, this misses the point of the accounts.

In addition to providing an historical record of the financial performance of the practice, the accounts are also a useful tool in making financial decisions. For example, the profit and loss account shows the profitability of the practice. If the GPs are earning low profits they can use the profit and loss account to see why this is, and what changes they need to make to improve their profits, for example, by trying to reduce expenditure.

Third parties may also want to see the accounts. For example, the bank may want to ensure that the practice is able to repay any loan commitments, or a potential new partner may want to assess the financial situation of the practice.

How often are accounts prepared?

The final accounts will usually be prepared annually, however accounts can be produced more often than once a year in order to give information to the GPs. For example, if a partner leaves the practice part way through the year, then a practice may decide to prepare the accounts for a shorter period to the date the partner left. This will enable them to calculate how much money that partner is owed from the practice.

Who prepares them and why?

Normally a practice will employ the services of a Chartered Accountant to produce their accounts and give them financial advice. However, there is no requirement for GPs to have their accounts audited, hence they may be produced by someone who is not a qualified accountant. This is because there is only a requirement for Limited and Public Limited Company (PLC) accounts to be audited. However, it is recommended that the accounts are produced by an independent firm of qualified accountants. Anyone can call themselves an accountant, but a qualified accountant will have undertaken training and exams to ensure they develop business awareness and professional judgement. Qualified accountants will be members of their professional institute and will be expected to maintain a high standard of ethical and professional conduct.

Chartered Accountant

A Chartered accountant is a qualified accountant who is a member of the Institute of Chartered Accountants in England and Wales. Someone who is a Chartered Accountant will have the letters ACA or FCA after their name.

Do accounts have to be prepared in a certain way?

The final accounts comprise the profit and loss account and the balance sheet, which are prepared from the practice's accounting records. The presentation of accounts will differ between accountants, however, there is a fairly standard layout for the profit and loss account and balance sheet.

For example, in the profit and loss account, income is normally shown at the top of the page. The expenses are shown next with the net profit at the bottom. (See Chapter 7 for *Different formats for accounts.*)

Chapter 2

Profit and loss account

The profit and loss account shows the income that the practice has received less (minus) the various expenses (overheads) incurred in running the practice for a given time period. The expenses are deducted from the income to give the net profit for that period.

Why is it important?

The profit and loss account is important because it shows the profitability of the practice. Profit means how much money has been earned from the day to day activities of running the practice.

- GPs are conducting a business, and the main object of a business is to maximise profits.
- New partners thinking about joining a practice will be interested in the profitability of the practice, as this will give them an indication of their likely earnings.
- The profits of the practice will need to be calculated, as this will need to be declared on the GP's tax return for the Inland Revenue.
- The practice's bank will also be interested in the profitability of the practice, to ensure that they are earning enough income to continue to repay any debts that they may have with the bank.

> ### Profit and loss
> The profit and loss account (sometimes known as the income and expenditure account) shows the income, expenses and net profit for a given time period.

Accounting period

The profit and loss account will cover the practice's accounting period. The accounting period will normally be 12 months to their year-end date. A practice's year-end date is normally decided when the practice commences trading and is usually 12 months after this date. In the example given in this chapter, the practice's year-end is 30 June. This means that they probably commenced trading as a practice some time in the past on the 1 July. Hence, the accounting period runs from 1 July to 30 June the following year.

If the accounting period does not cover 12 months, the accounts should clearly state what period they cover. This would normally be shown on the front page of the accounts, for example 'For the period from 1 July to 31 December'.

It should be noted that accounting periods may be different to the tax year, which runs from 6 April to 5 April the following year (see Chapter 10 *Taxation and superannuation*).

Comparative figures

The accounts should also include comparative figures from the previous accounting period. In the example shown at the end of this chapter, the profit and loss account shows the figures for 12 months to 30 June 2004 and the previous 12 months to 30 June 2003. This allows the practice to compare the current year's figures to the previous year's and identify any discrepancies that may need investigation. For example, telephone costs for the year ended 30 June 2003 were £2975 and for the year ended 30 June 2004 this increased to £4117. The practice may want to know what caused the sudden increase and what they can do to reduce this expense for the year to 30 June 2005.

Income

The income that the practice has earned will be shown at the top of the profit and loss account. Different accountants will present the income in different ways (see Chapter 7 *Different formats for accounts*).

The example shows three headings for income:
- Fees earned
- Reimbursements
- Other income

An analysis of these headings is shown separately on additional pages called 'Schedules' or 'Notes' (in this case, Schedules 1, 2 and 3). To summarise, this income is as follows:
- *Fees earned* – this is the total figure of the income earned from GMS or PMS for the care of the practice's patients (see Chapter 9 for an explanation of how practices are paid).
- *Reimbursements* – this is the total figure of the reimbursements the practice has received towards the cost of running the practice (see Chapter 9 for an explanation of how practices are paid).
- *Other income* – this is the total figure of other income that the practice has earned, for example, income from writing medical reports.

The example shows that the practice has earned £611,679 of income for the 12 months to 30 June 2004. In the previous 12 months the practice earned £520,609 of income.

Overheads / expenses

Overheads are the expenses that are incurred in the day-to-day running of the practice, for example, salaries and wages of the practice staff. In this example the expenses are listed. Again, different accountants may present the expenses in different ways.

Overheads / expenses

These words mean the same thing. Some accountants may use the word overheads, others may use the word expenses.

The example shows the practice incurred expenses of £281,415 for the 12 months to 30 June 2004. The comparative expenses for the 12 months to 30 June 2003 were £264,506.

Brackets

Figures in brackets mean that they are deducted from another figure to give a total. For example, the figure for total expenses of £281,415 is in brackets as it is deducted from the income of £611,679 to give the net profit of £330,264.

Net profit

Income less the expenses give the practice's net profit for the period. This is the net income the practice has earned after paying the expenses. The net profit is important as it shows the profitability of the practice. In this example, the practice earned a net profit of £330,264 for 12 months to 30 June 2004. The comparative net profit for the 12 months to 30 June 2003 was £256,103.

Net profit or gross profit

Accountants may talk about gross profit and net profit.

Gross profit. For a trading business which buy goods at one price and then sells the same goods at a higher price, the difference between the two represents a profit which is known as the gross profit. This is the profit on the sale of these goods. For example, if I purchase an item for £10 and then sell the same item for £15, the gross profit would be £5.

This part of the profit and loss account is shown at the top and starts with the income received from the sale of these items, then the cost of these items (known as 'cost of sales') is deducted. The difference is the gross profit. This would only appear for GPs in a practice which is a dispensing practice; they would buy drugs and the cost of the drugs would be shown as the 'cost of sales', and then these drugs would be dispensed which would generate income, and the difference between the income and cost of sales is the gross profit. The profit and loss would continue with other income received less the

---

overheads of the practice, which would finally give the overall net profit of the practice.

Net profit. The net profit is the final profit that the business has made, after deducting all the expenses incurred in running the business.

The net profit is the amount which is then shared by the partners to give their individual earnings for the year (see Chapter 4 *Profit allocation*).

If the partners want to increase the amount that they earn they need to increase the profitability of the practice. To increase profitability a practice needs to increase the income earned and/or reduce the practice expenses incurred.

Notes to the accounts

The accounts themselves are two pages, the profit and loss account and the balance sheet. All other pages and information are subordinate to these pages. On these two pages there will be reference to 'Notes' or 'Schedules'; the two words are often used interchangeably. These are additional pages, which explain further about a figure on the profit and loss or balance sheet. In this case the accounts include both Schedules of income and Notes. The Schedules is the format that is used by this particular accountant.

Understanding Practice Accounts

DR SLAVIN AND PARTNERS
PROFIT AND LOSS ACCOUNT
FOR THE YEAR ENDED 30 JUNE 2004

	Sch	2004 £	2004 £	2003 £	2003 £
Fees earned (before deduction of £21,521 Superannuation)	1		382,856		309,850
Reimbursements	2		179,147		171,711
Other Income	3		49,676		39,048
			611,679		520,609
LESS OVERHEADS					
Salaries and Wages		139,088		139,550	
GP Registrar		17,877		–	
Staff Welfare		2323		2947	
Staff Pension		11,201		8901	
Locums		–		100	
Deputising Service		15,008		18,313	
Drugs		8115		13,148	
Medical Supplies and Instruments		1657		1662	
Telephone		4117		2975	
Computer Expenses		5003		6221	
Printing, Postage and Stationery		6781		5763	
Books and Journals		–		145	
General Expenses		402		435	
Training Fund Expenses		6970		2384	
Company Health Insurance		4033		3338	
Courses and Conferences		–		145	
Repairs and Maintenance		2314		4833	
Heat and Light		3466		2672	
Cleaning		6234		5012	
Insurance		1514		1129	
Rates		4858		4655	
Levies		2034		1465	
Bank Interest and Charges		327		811	
Bank Loan Interest		–		211	
Mortgage Interest		27,556		26,024	
Legal and Professional Fees		–		748	
Accountancy		4935		4700	
Depreciation		5602		6219	
			(281,415)		(264,506)
NET PROFIT FOR THE YEAR (NOTE 1)			330,264		256,103

Chapter 3

Balance sheet

The profit and loss account shows the income and expenses for the accounting period, and usually covers a 12 month period. In contrast, the balance sheet shows the values of the assets and liabilities on a single day. Hence, the balance sheet represents a snapshot of the practice's finances. This day will usually be the practice's year end date.

Assets and liabilities

Assets are items or amounts that the practice own or are owed to them. For example, if they own the premises, this is an asset. The money in the bank account is also an asset. The assets can be divided into 'fixed' and 'current' assets. Fixed assets represent long term assets (often the premises). Current assets represent short term assets (such as cash). Liabilities are amounts that the practice owes. For example, the mortgage for the premises is a liability, as it is owed to the lender.

There are two halves to the balance sheet. The top half lists the value of all the assets and liabilities of the practice and the bottom half shows how much each partner owns of these assets. The partners' share of assets can be shown as a capital and current account. The value of the assets and liabilities (top half of the balance sheet) is the same value as the capital and current accounts (bottom half of the balance sheet) – hence the term balance sheet.

> ### Capital and current accounts
>
> The terms 'capital account' and 'current account' are generally interchangeable and refer to the wealth of the practice. The total of a partner's capital and current account is the amount of money they have invested in the practice and it will be this amount that they are entitled to when they leave. In this case, the capital account is used to show a partner's share of the net equity. However, not all accountants do this, some show the capital account as a fixed amount which the partners have agreed.

The balance sheet should also include comparative figures showing the value of the assets at the previous year-end date. In the example shown in this chapter, the balance sheet is a snapshot of the value of assets and liabilities at 30 June 2004. The comparative shows the value at 30 June 2003.

Fixed assets

Fixed assets are those assets that are long term and have a lifespan of more than 12 months. These include fixtures and fittings, office and medical equipment, premises, etc. Fixed assets are divided into tangible and intangible assets:

- *Tangible assets* will be the premises (if owned), fixtures, fittings, and office and medical equipment. The value of the premises on the balance sheet may be represented by either the original cost to purchase or build the property, or the value of the property on the open market. The open market value is the value that the practice would receive if they sold the premises. In this example the premises are shown at the market value three years ago, which is £450,000. The mortgage on the property of £425,278 is then deducted from the value to give the net equity of £24,722. The mortgage amount is in brackets as it is a liability and is deducted from the value of the premises. The value of the other tangible assets (fixtures, fittings, equipment, etc.) in the accounts will be the net book value. (See Chapter 5 *Other tangible assets* for an explanation of how other tangibles assets are valued and depreciated.)
- *Intangible assets* are assets which do not have a physical, tangible existence, for example, goodwill.

> **Net equity**
> This is the difference between the value of the premises and the balance outstanding on the mortgage. If a practice is in negative equity, it means that their mortgage is higher than the value of the premises.

Current assets

Current assets, are short term assets which can be turned into cash in the next 12 months. These include stock of drugs, debtors (see below) and bank funds. The value of these will change from day to day. For example, the money in the bank account will change due to income being received and overheads being paid.

Current assets will be made up of the following:

Stock

This will be the value of the stock of drugs at the year-end. Normally the drugs left at the year-end will be counted and valued. In this example, there is not much stock left at the year-end so this has not been valued and treated as an asset. Because general practice accounts are not required to be prepared in a particular format like limited companies, quite often if stock of drugs is only a couple of hundred pounds it is not included in the accounts.

Sundry debtors

Debtors comprise money that is owed from third parties to the practice. The practice will have completed this work within the accounting period but not yet received payment for it. For example, medical reports may have been written and sent to solicitors, but the income may not be received until after the year-end. In this example, the sundry debtors are £22,006, which means that the practice is owed this amount of money and it should be received in the bank account after the year-end, i.e. after 30 June 2004.

Prepayments

These represent expenses that have been prepaid for a particular period. For example, a practice may pay the building and contents insurance in January 2004 to cover the whole year up to 31 December 2004. If their year-end is 30 June 2004, they would have paid from 1 July 2004 to 31 December 2004 in advance – the amount for that period would be treated as being prepaid.

Bank balance

This will be the reconciled bank balance at the year-end. Reconciled means the balance at the year-end less any cheques that were written in the accounting period, but have not cleared the bank at the year-end. If the bank account is overdrawn this will be shown under current liabilities. A bank account that is overdrawn means that the practice owes money to the bank. (Note that this is represented as a liability, rather than being in brackets under current assets.) In this example, the reconciled bank balance is £62,028.

Cash in hand

This will be the amount of cash that is left in the petty cash tin at the year-end. In this example, the amount of cash left at 30 June 2004 is £279.

Current liabilities

Current liabilities are amounts that are owed to a third party at the year-end date and are payable within 12 months and they usually comprise:

Sundry creditors and accruals

This is the amount owed to third parties at the year-end. For example, drugs purchased during the accounting period, but not paid for by the time of the year-end. In this example, the sundry creditors outstanding at 30 June 2004 are £68,786.

Bank loan

If the practice has a bank loan then the outstanding balance due at the year-end would be shown under current liabilities. The mortgage for the premises would not be shown as a current liability as this is a long-term loan. The reason for this is that current liabilities are those liabilities which are payable within 12 months, whereas a mortgage is likely to repayable over a much longer period, so would normally be shown as a long term liability. In this example the mortgage is offset against the value of the property at the top of the balance sheet; this accountant shows it this way so the practice can clearly see what the net equity is in the property.

Net current assets

The total of the current liabilities are deducted from the current assets to give the net current assets. In this example the total current liabilities is £68,786, which is deducted from the total current assets of £84,313 to give the net current assets of £15,527.

The net current assets are then added to the fixed assets. In this example, the net assets of £15,527 are added to the total fixed assets of £47,634 to give the total assets (less liabilities) of £63,161.

So what does the £63,161 mean to a practice? In effect, it is the amount of money that they would have left if they sold all their assets and paid off all their liabilities at the date the balance sheet has been prepared.

If the partners decided to dissolve the practice on the 30 June 2004 and sold the property for £450,000, then paid off the mortgage of £425,278, the net amount remaining of £24,722 would increase the bank balance. If the tangible assets were sold for the value on the balance sheet, the bank account would increase by a further £22,912. The practice would receive the debtors (money owed to them) and this would increase the bank account by £22,006. They would have to pay their creditors (money owed by them), which would reduce the bank balance by £68,786. After all of these transactions the bank account balance would be £63,161, this would not simply be split equally between the partners, but would be split depending on who owned the assets.

Who owns the assets?

The bottom half of the balance sheet shows the ownership of the practice by way of capital accounts and current accounts. Each partner's share of the wealth is shown in his or her individual capital account and current account. This is their investment in the practice and would be the cash to which they are entitled, should they leave (see Chapter 6 *Capital and current accounts* for a further explanation of capital and current accounts).

In the example of this balance sheet, Dr Perry has a balance on her capital account of £6982 and has an overdrawn balance on her current account of £10,406; the overdrawn balance means she owes the practice this amount of money. Therefore, if she left the practice at 30 June 2004 and sold her share of the property, she would owe the practice £3424 (£10,406 – £6982). If she left the practice, but kept her share of the property as an investment, then she would owe the practice £10,406; she would not be paid her capital account as this represents her share of the equity in the property and, as she is not selling her share of the property, she is not entitled to her share of equity.

DR SLAVIN AND PARTNERS
BALANCE SHEET
AS AT 30 JUNE 2004

	Note	2004		2003	
		£	£	£	£
FIXED ASSETS					
Property			450,000		450,000
Less: Mortgage			(425,278)		(425,278)
Net Equity			24,722		24,722
Other Tangible Assets	2		22,912		28,514
			47,634		53,236
CURRENT ASSETS					
Sundry Debtors and Prepayments		22,006		85,396	
Main Bank Account		62,028		30,803	
Cash in Hand		279		108	
		84,313		116,307	
CURRENT LIABILITIES					
Sundry Creditors and Accruals		68,786		64,430	
NET CURRENT ASSETS			15,527		51,877
TOTAL ASSETS			63,161		105,113

Above this line is the top half of the balance sheet

Below this line is the bottom half of the balance sheet
The total of the top half and the bottom half balance, hence the name 'balance sheet'

	Note	2004		2003	
REPRESENTED BY:					
CAPITAL ACCOUNTS	3				
Dr Slavin		6982		6982	
Dr Singer		10,758		10,758	
Dr Perry		6982		6982	
			24,722		24,722
CURRENT ACCOUNTS	4				
Dr Slavin		25,951		37,763	
Dr Singer		23,567		29,294	
Dr Perry		(10,406)		13,334	
Dr Stone		(673)		–	
			38,439		80,391
			63,161		105,113

Notes

Beside other tangible assets is a number 2, this is under the column headed Note. This means that the figure of £22,912 is explained further in Note 2 of the accounts; all Notes follow on additional sheets after the balance sheet.

Chapter 4

Profit allocation

The partners in the practice are entitled to a share of profits; this is the net income they have earned for the period. The profit allocation shows how the net profit for the period is shared amongst the partners.

Prior allocation

The profits of the practice are shared according to the profit sharing ratios. However, there may be some income or expenses which is not shared in the profit sharing ratios. For example, most practices allocate seniority to the partner it relates to. This would need to be prior allocated to the relevant partner first before the balance of profits is shared amongst the partners.

Profit sharing ratios

The profit sharing ratios (PSR) are the ratios in which a partnership shares the net profit.

Examples of prior allocations include:
- *Notional and cost rent income.* This income should only be allocated to the partners that own the surgery premises. If all the partners own the premises, it may be owned in different proportions to the profit sharing ratios. Therefore, this income would be allocated in the proportions that the partners own the premises. For example, a three partner practice may split profits in the ratio of 40: 40: 20, but they

may own the property equally – the property-related income would be shared equally and not in the ratio 40: 40: 20.

Notional / cost rent

Practices have to work out of premises and are therefore eligible for reimbursements which relate to renting or owning their premises.

If the practice owns their premises they will either be reimbursed on a cost rent or notional rent basis (see Chapter 9 *How GPs get paid* for more information).

- *Mortgage interest.* As this expense relates to the interest on the mortgage for the premises, it should be allocated to the partners who own the surgery premises and in the proportions that they own it. Because this is an expense, it should be deducted from the partners' shares of profits, and will be shown in brackets.
- *Seniority.* Seniority is paid to the practice to reward partners for their service to the NHS. The amount the practice receives depends on the number of years each partner has served. As mentioned earlier, because this income is for the individual partner it is usually allocated to the partner that it relates to and not shared in the profit sharing ratios.

In the example shown in this chapter, Dr Slavin has £7969 of income as a prior allocation, Dr Singer £7160, Dr Perry £6562 and Dr Stone £2656. This income is paid to the individual partners in addition to their share of the profits.

Profits shared in profit sharing ratios

Once the prior allocation has been calculated, the balance of profits will be shared in the profit sharing ratios. The profit sharing ratios reflect the amount of time each partner spends in the practice. The profit sharing ratios can be calculated based on the number of sessions each partner does, or whether they are full time or part time. All partners should agree the profit sharing ratios. This would usually be recorded as part of the partnership agreement – however, the profit sharing ratios may change from year to year as partners may decide to alter the number of sessions they work.

During the year there may be changes in the profit sharing ratios; for example, a full time partner may decide to reduce their hours to be part time; a partner may leave the practice; or a new partner may join during the year. When these events occur the profit sharing ratios will need to be revised to reflect these changes.

Where there is a change in profit sharing ratios, the profits earned before and after the change need to be apportioned appropriately. This is done by assuming that profits accrue evenly throughout the year. In this example, Drs Slavin, Singer and Perry shared profits equally up to 31 July 2003. Dr Stone joined as a partner on 1 August 2003 and the revised profit sharing ratios were 4 : 4 : 3 : 2.55. From 1 February 2004 the ratios changed again to 4 : 4 : 3 : 3. The ratios changed because Dr Stone is a new partner and from 1 August to 31 January, Dr Stone was on an 85% parity share of profits and then from 1 February was on a full parity share. It is common practice that when a new partner joins a partnership they do not receive a full share of profits. Initially, they will earn between 80–90% parity. In this example, Dr Stone's full parity share is 3, so 85% parity is calculated as $3 \times 85\%$ which equals 2.55.

The total profits for the year are £330,264. An amount of £24,347 has been prior allocated to the partners, leaving a balance of £305,917 to be shared in the profit sharing ratios. As there are changes in the ratios during the year the balance needs to be split into the different periods, as follows:

- *The first period.* This occurs from the start of the accounting year to the date of the first change, i.e. 1 July 2003 to 31 July 2003, this is 31 days. As profits are assumed to accrue evenly, the amount of profit for this period is calculated as 31 days divided by 366 days (2004 was a leap year) and the result is multiplied by the balance of profits of £305,917. This gives a profit figure for the 31 days of £25,911; this is then split in the profit sharing ratios for this period.
- *The second period.* The next period is from 1 August 2003 to 31 January 2004 and again profits would need to be calculated and shared, based on the relevant profits sharing ratios.

This process is repeated until all profits are shared.

For each partner their prior allocation plus their share of the balance is added together to give their total share of profits for the period. In this example:

- Dr Slavin has received a total share of profits of £98,067 (this is made up of £7969 [prior allocation] + £8637 + £45,400 + £36,061)
- Dr Singer has received £97,258
- Dr Perry has received £76,294
- Dr Stone has received £58,645

The partner's share of profits, after adjustments for tax purposes, is the amount that they will pay tax on.

Adjustments to profits for tax

For tax purposes, adjustments may need to be made to the calculated profits. This is because some income or expenses may not be allowable for tax purposes. For example, depreciation of the assets is shown as an expense in the profit and loss account, but depreciation is not allowed for tax. However, capital allowances can be claimed on the assets instead of depreciation. The reason for this is that depreciation rates are usually decided by the accountants, whereas the rates for capital allowances are set by the Inland Revenue (see Chapter 10 *Taxation and superannuation*).

DR SLAVIN AND PARTNERS
NOTES TO THE ACCOUNTS
FOR THE YEAR ENDED 30 JUNE 2004

1. ALLOCATION OF PROFIT

	Dr Slavin	Dr Singer	Dr Perry	Dr Stone	Total
	£	£	£	£	£
Prior allocation					
Notional rent	11,992	11,992	11,992	–	35,976
Mortgage interest	(8991)	(9456)	(9109)	–	(27,556)
Building insurance	(253)	(253)	(253)	–	(759)
PGEA	1763	2195	2661	2656	9275
Seniority	1328	552	221	–	2101
Private fees	2130	2130	1050	–	5310
	7969	7160	6562	2656	24,347
Balance					
1 July 2003 – 31 July 2003 (31/366)					
PSR – Equal split	8637	8637	8637	–	25,911
1 Aug 2003 – 31 Jan 2004 (184/366)					
PSR – 4 : 4 : 3 : 2.55	45,400	45,400	34,050	28,944	153,794
1 Feb 2004 – 30 June 2004 (151/366)					
PSR – 4 : 4 : 3 : 3	36,061	36,061	27,045	27,045	126,212
	90,098	90,098	69,732	55,989	305,917
Total profit	98,067	97,258	76,294	58,645	330,264

Chapter 5

Other tangible fixed assets

Other tangible assets are those assets that have a lifespan of more than 12 months, for example, computer equipment, fixtures and fittings, and medical equipment (this chapter excludes premises as these are shown separately on the balance sheet – if there is a supporting note it would be called Property). The initial costs of purchasing these assets are not treated as a one-off expense in the profit and loss account. Because the useful economic life of these assets extends for longer than the 12 months of the accounting period, they appear as capital (capitalised on the balance sheet). However, in subsequent accounts they are 'written off' over the agreed period of their economic life.

It is necessary for the balance sheet to reflect the realistic value of the assets at the accounting year-end. The value of the fixed assets will reduce over time, due to the effect of wear and tear on that asset – this is known as depreciation.

Depreciation and writing off

The reduction in the value of an asset due to wear and tear is measured by what is known as depreciation. The amount of depreciation between accounting years is the amount by which the asset has been written off. Depreciation is a way of writing off the cost of the asset over its useful economic life. Depreciation is shown as an expense in the profit and loss account each year.

For example, if a computer was purchased in 2003 for £1000 and its useful economic life is estimated at

> 4 years, then the value of the asset would reduce by £250 (£1000 divided by 4) per year. This amount is the depreciation and would be shown as an expense in the profit and loss account for each of the 4 years.

In the example at the end of this chapter, the value of the other tangible assets shown on the balance sheet at 30 June 2004 is £22,912; this is known as the net book value. There should always be a note in the accounts that shows how the net book value has been calculated. The note should show the original cost, depreciation and the net book value of the assets.

Net book value

The net book value is the original cost of the asset less the depreciation that has been charged to date. The net book value is an estimate of the value of the asset if sold at the accounting year end. In the example of the computer above, the computer would have a net book value of £500 in 2005 – having had two annual depreciation sums of £250 deducted from its original cost.

Cost

The note relating to net book value should begin by showing the original cost of the assets, which has been brought forward at the start of the year. This would be the accumulated cost of all assets that the practice has purchased. In this example, the original cost at 1 July 2003 for the computer equipment was £8433 and for the office equipment £61,767. If the practice had purchased any assets during the accounting period this would be shown separately as additions in the year as follows:

	Computer Equipment	Office Equipment	Total
Cost at 1 July 2003	8433	61,767	70,200
Additions	800	2,000	2800
Cost at 30 June 2004	9233	63,767	73,000

However, in the example at the end of this chapter (Note 2: Other tangible fixed assets) there were no additions in the accounting period. Therefore the cost of the assets was the same at the start and end of the accounting period.

Depreciation

Depreciation is calculated each year to take account of the wear and tear of the assets. The note shows the depreciation at the start of the accounting period. This is the accumulated depreciation or the total depreciation which has been deducted (charged) in the previous accounting periods. In this example, the accumulated depreciation at 1 July 2003 for computer equipment was £3214 and for office equipment was £38,472.

The next line is the depreciation charge for the accounting period, which is shown as the 'charge for the year'. Depreciation is calculated using either the straight line method or the reducing balance method. Accountants will decide upon what percentage to use to depreciate an asset. In this example the computer equipment is depreciated using 25% straight line method, however, another accountant may use 20%. The reason that there is not a set rule on depreciating assets is that depreciation is not an allowable expense for tax purposes. Instead, capital allowances are claimed and there are set rules for these which are given by the Inland Revenue.

Charge for year

The charge for the year is the amount of depreciation which is shown in the profit and loss account as an expense.

Straight line depreciation

In this example, the depreciation charge for the year for computer equipment is calculated based on 25% straight line. This means that 25% of the cost is classed as depreciation in each full year, which is equivalent to £2108. This amount is added to the accumulated depreciation at 1 July 2003 to give the accumulated depreciation at 30 June 2004.

Reducing balance depreciation

The depreciation charge for the office equipment is 15% reducing balance. This is calculated by deducting the accumulated depreciation at 1 July 2003 from the cost at 30 June

2004 and multiplying by 15%, which is equivalent to £3494 (cost is £61,767 − depreciation of £38,472 = £23,295 × 15% = £3494).

The total depreciation charge for the year of £5602 is shown in the profit and loss account as an expense.

Net book value

In this example, the computer equipment's original cost was £8433, and it has been depreciated by £5322 to give a net book value at 30 June 2004 of £3111. If the practice wanted to sell the computer equipment, this should represent the likely value they would receive for it. The office equipment's original cost was £61,767, and it has been depreciated by £41,966 to give a net book value at 30 June 2004 of £19,801.

The note also shows the net book value at the previous accounting year-end. This is the cost less the accumulated depreciation at the start of the accounting period. In this example, the total cost of the assets at 1 July 2003 was £70,200, less the accumulated depreciation at 1 July 2003 of £41,686, giving a net book value of £28,514.

Other tangible fixed assets

DR. SLAVIN AND PARTNERS
NOTES TO THE ACCOUNTS
FOR THE YEAR ENDED 30 JUNE 2004

2. OTHER TANGIBLE FIXED ASSETS

	Computer Equipment	Office Equipment	Total
	£	£	£
Cost			
At 1 July 2003 and at 30 June 2004	8,433	61,767	70,200
Depreciation			
At 1 July 2003	3,214	38,472	41,686
Charge for the year	2,108	3494	5602
At 30 June 2004	5,322	41,966	47,288
Net Book Values			
At 30 June 2004	3,111	19,801	22,912
At 30 June 2003	5,219	23,295	28,514

Chapter 6

Capital and current accounts

This is the least well understood part of the partnership accounts, but it is extremely important, as it represents real wealth, and will translate into cash when there is a change in the partnership.

The terms 'capital account' and 'current account' are generally interchangeable and refer to the wealth of the practice. The amount in each partner's capital and current account is, in effect, their investment in the practice and would be the cash to which they are entitled should they leave the practice. The investment is used to finance the purchase of assets for the practice such as property and fixtures and fittings, and also the money in the bank account to meet the day to day running of the practice.

Capital accounts

If a practice owns their surgery premises and the cost of the property is included in the accounts, then the equity in the property is usually shown separately as a capital account for the partners who own the premises. The net equity of the premises will be the value of the property less the related mortgage. In this example, the net equity of the property is £24,722 (see Chapter 3 on the *Balance sheet*).

Quite often, the property is owned in different shares to the profit sharing ratios, or not all of the partners will own a share of the property. It is important that the balance sheet clearly shows who owns the property and what their share is.

In this example, only Dr Slavin, Dr Singer and Dr Perry own the property; Drs Slavin and Perry own a 28% share each, and Dr Singer owns a 44% share. This ratio is different to the ratio in which they share the profits. Each partner has a capital account to the value of his or her share of the net equity in the property. Drs Slavin and Perry's share of the net equity is £6982 each and Dr Singer's share is £10,758. If the property were to be sold at the balance sheet date, these would be the amounts they would each receive from the sale after the mortgage is repaid.

When there is a change in the value of the net equity in the property (i.e. payments have been made to repay mortgage capital), then a transfer is normally made from the partners' current accounts to the capital accounts. This is done to ensure that the capital accounts are always equivalent to the equity in the property. However, if the property is revalued, this is accounted for by increasing the value of the property on the balance sheet to the revalued amount. Hence, this would increase each partner's capital account.

Current accounts

The current accounts of each individual partner show their share of profits less drawings.

Drawings

A partner's individual current account shows their share of profits less their total drawings. Drawings not only includes the amount they have been paid each month, but also includes the taxation and superannuation that has been paid by the practice on their behalf.

Current account values are increased by profit earned and decreased by drawings. A partner is entitled to draw their share of profits from the practice, but if their drawings are more than their share of profits, then their current account would reduce and possibly go overdrawn.

It is important to appreciate that drawings include not only cash or cheques taken by each partner each month, but also payments made by the practice on behalf of a partner, such as for superannuation, added years, and taxation. Two partners sharing profits equally may well have different superannuation payments, perhaps due to one partner buying added years, and they will almost certainly have differing tax liabilities. This would mean in reality that they should take differing amounts of monthly drawings to ensure that, at the end of the year, their respective shares of the wealth are equal.

The balance on each partner's current account would be the money they were entitled to should they leave the practice. If the balance is shown in brackets (i.e. they had overdrawn) then this amount would need to be repaid to the practice as it means that the partner has taken more money from the practice than they are entitled to. This may have happened if profits are lower in the year than expected. Profits will not be known until the final accounts have been produced, so the partners' drawings are estimated based on expected profits. If the amount they have drawn is less than the actual profits, the partners may decide to draw out a portion of available balance. However, they would still need to leave a small amount in the practice to meet the day to day running expenses.

The current accounts note shows the balance at the start of the accounting period. This is the accumulated amount of money that each partner has not drawn over time. The balance at the start of the accounting period for Drs Slavin, Singer and Perry is £37,763, £29,294 and £13,334, respectively. Dr Stone does not have a balance at the start of the accounting period as she only joined as a partner in the accounting period ended 30 June 2004.

The individual partners' share of profits for the accounting period is added to the balance at the start of the accounting period. Dr Slavin's share of profits for the year ended 30 June 2004 is £98,067 (this is made up of prior allocated income of £7969 and a balance of profits of £90,098 – see Chapter 4 *Profit allocation*), and this is added to his balance at 1 July 2003 of £37,763 to give total income available to draw of £135,830.

The next part to the note is the deduction of total drawings from the income available to draw. Total drawings would include the amounts taken each month for superannuation and taxation (if the practice pays this). For Dr Slavin, his monthly drawings for the year totalled £105,140 and the practice had paid superannuation on his behalf of £4739, and so his total drawings for the year were £109,879. This amount is deducted from the total profits and then added to his balance at 1 July 2003 (£135,830) to leave a balance on his current account at 30 June 2004 of £25,951. If Dr Slavin left at 30 June 2004, he would be entitled to this amount, as it is equivalent to his profits not yet taken.

Dr Singer has a balance on his current account of £23,567 and Dr Perry has an overdrawn current account of £10,406; Dr Stone also has an overdrawn current account of £673. Dr Perry and Dr Stone would need to repay these amounts back to the practice. This could be done, for instance, by taking reduced drawings for the next year. The practice accountants would need to advise the partners how much they could draw to ensure that their individual balances on their current accounts did not go overdrawn in future.

Overdrawn current account

If a partner's current account is overdrawn this will be shown in brackets. This means that the partner has drawn more money than they are entitled to. This money is owed back to the practice.

A new partner joining the practice would sometimes be asked to introduce some capital into the practice so they have a balance on their current account. If a new partner does not put capital into the practice, they will need to take reduced drawings so that they are building up a current account balance throughout the year.

It is important that the balances on the current account reflect each partner's commitment to the practice. It is fairly common to see accounts with differing current balances in spite of equal profit shares. For example, partners may share profits in a 50:50 ratio, but one is overdrawn and the other has a high positive balance. This is usually a result of poor financial advice. This situation should not be ignored, as the balances will translate into cash as and when a partner leaves, retires or dies.

DR. SLAVIN AND PARTNERS
NOTES TO THE ACCOUNTS
FOR THE YEAR ENDED 30 JUNE 2004

3. CAPITAL ACCOUNTS

	Dr Slavin	Dr Singer	Dr Perry	Total
	£	£	£	£
Balance at 1 July 2003 and at 30 June 2004	6982	10,758	6982	24,722

4. CURRENT ACCOUNTS

	Dr Slavin	Dr Singer	Dr Perry	Dr Stone	Total
	£	£	£	£	£
Balance at 1 July 2003	37,763	29,294	13,334	–	80,391
Share of Profit	98,067	97,258	76,294	58,645	330,264
	135,830	126,552	89,628	58,645	410,655
Less:					
Drawings	105,140	98,257	90,999	56,368	350,764
Superannuation	4739	4728	591	2,950	16,077
Added Years	–	–	5444	–	5444
	109,879	112,985	100,034	59,318	372,216
Balance at 30 June 2004	25,951	23,567	(10,406)	(673)	38,439

35

Chapter 7

Different formats for accounts

There is no statutory requirement for GPs to have their accounts audited (an auditor would be given a set of accounts produced by the client; the auditor would then need to carry out sample checks to satisfy themselves that the accounts give a true and fair view of the financial status of the partnership). The practice accountants will normally prepare accounts on behalf of the practice. The way a set of accounts is presented will depend on the accountant. The profit and loss account and balance sheet are standard pages in a set of accounts and therefore will be of a similar format. Some accountants may only prepare these two pages, while other accountants may produce more detailed accounts to give the practice as much information as possible.

To some GPs the main purpose of accounts is simply to calculate the profit to declare to the tax office. A simple profit and loss account and balance sheet will meet this objective. However, the accounts should provide the practice with a useful tool to enable them to make financial decisions.

Profit and loss account

The profit and loss account format will start with income at the top of the page and the expenses will be listed further down. Some accountants may only show one line for total income received. This serves little purpose to a practice, as this will not help to identify areas of income that they need to increase or to ensure that the correct amount of income has been received.

The accounts used in this book are prepared by medical specialist accountants, Ramsay, Brown and Partners. The income is shown at the top of the profit and loss account and is then analysed in detail on the schedule of income pages. With this format, a practice can see exactly what income they have received during the year. The accountant will use this detail to help the practice look at areas where income could be improved.

The expenses will normally be listed on the profit and loss accounts. However, some accountants will then analyse this figure further on other pages of the accounts. Examples of expense categories would be salaries and wages, premises costs, and administration costs. The breakdown would then be shown on separate pages to the accounts.

If a figure in the accounts is analysed further, it should clearly show a note/schedule number beside it, which means you can find further information on how this figure has been arrived at.

Balance sheet

The layout of the balance sheet will usually be of standard format. The only difference will be how the bottom half of the balance sheet is presented. This is the partners' capital. Some accountants may only show current accounts even though the property is owned by the partners. It is important that the equity in the property is shown separately as capital accounts, if not, this can cause problems when a partner leaves.

For example, let's assume that a GP who retires from the partnership decides to keep his share of the property as an investment. As he is not selling his share, he is not entitled to his share of the equity. If his current account was £30,000 and this comprised his share of equity and working capital, he would still want to be paid out his share of the working capital as he is no longer a partner. Problems can arise where, let's say, the £30,000 is made up of £40,000 net equity and a deficit in working capital of £10,000. As the partner is keeping his share of the property he would need to repay the partnership the deficit of £10,000 as this means he has taken more money out of the practice than he had earned. If his share of the net equity had been shown separately as a capital account of £30,000 and his current account as negative £10,000 then it would be clear that he had an overdrawn current account which he could have repaid by reducing his drawings while a partner in the practice, instead of being asked to repay this money once he had left.

Profit allocation

The profit allocation is very important as it shows each partner exactly how their profits have been calculated. There is no standard format for this and it is possible to see accounts without this page. Any GP looking at this page should be able to clearly see what income and or expenses have been prior allocated, and how the balance has been shared out and in what ratio.

Tangible assets

The layout for tangible assets shown is standard amongst accountants. The only difference will be that different accountants will use different rates to calculate depreciation.

Chapter 8

Medical specialist accounts

The accounts used in this book are prepared by medical specialist accountants. The book has so far covered the main pages that will be found in a set of accounts:

- Profit and loss account
- Balance sheet
- Profit allocation
- Tangible asset note
- Capital and current account notes

This present chapter looks at the other pages that may be included in medical accounts, and describes how this additional information can assist practices in making financial decisions.

Schedules of income

This particular medical accountant analyses income received in the 'Schedules of income' pages. These schedules show the practice's income, line by line so that the partners can see exactly what they have received. This allows a practice to see where they can improve their income and to ensure that they have been correctly paid for the services provided.

- Schedule 1 details the income earned for providing services to their patients

- Schedule 2 details the reimbursements that the practice has received
- Schedule 3 details all other income that the practice has received
- Schedules 4 and 5 detail how much has been received for each area of the quality and outcomes framework
- Schedule 6 details how much the practice has received for enhanced services provided

Practice statistics

Accounts prepared by medical specialist accountants are likely to include ratios and analysis, which help provide a practice with information on how they are performing, compared to an 'average practice'. Ratio analysis can be used to highlight to a practice where they need to make improvements so that they can increase the profits of the practice. For example, the accountants may look at the practice's level of expenses compared to an average practice, or the levels of income earned compared to an average practice.

The values for the 'average practice' are calculated based on the data available within the accountant's clients rather than published averaged figures.

DR SLAVIN AND PARTNERS
SCHEDULES OF INCOME
FOR THE YEAR ENDED 30 JUNE 2004

	Sch	2004	2003
SCHEDULE 1		£	£
Fees Earned			
Fixed Income			
Capitation Fees		116,789	149,611
Basic Practice Allowance		26,039	31,532
Deprivation Payments		10,577	12,259
Out of Hours Allowance		7819	10,079
Postgraduate Education Allowance		9275	8415
Effort Related Income			
Targets, Vaccinations			
Age 2 : High		7784	9349
: Low		–	–
Age 5 : High		2950	2573
: Low		–	272
Targets, Cytology : High		7943	10,501
: Low		–	–
Items of Service	4	36,262	47,183
Child Health Surveillance		4313	5100
Registration Fees		10,033	3611
Health Promotion		7442	9853
Asthma Management		–	–
Diabetes Management		1413	1820
Minor Surgery		3170	3680
Quality Allowance		1805	2913
GMS Uplift		3064	–
Old GMS Contract		256,678	308,751
Global Sum		84,065	–
		340,743	308,751
MPIG Correction Factor		18,568	–
Seniority		2101	1099
		361,412	309,850
Quality and Outcome Framework	5	19,237	–
Enhanced Services	6	2207	–
		382,856	309,850

DR SLAVIN AND PARTNERS
SCHEDULES OF INCOME
FOR THE YEAR ENDED 30 JUNE 2004

	2004	2003
SCHEDULE 2	£	£
Reimbursements		
Staff (9 months)	87,054	110,244
GP Registrar	17,877	–
Rent and Rates	40,700	38,600
Computer Expenses	5534	2509
Drugs	16,858	20,358
Quality Preparation	11,124	–
	179,147	171,711
SCHEDULE 3		
Other Income		
Private Fees	18,676	17,951
Training Fund	6970	2384
Quality Information Preparation Payment	3657	–
Nursing Homes	–	900
Other HA Income	828	419
Training Grant	2689	–
Primary Care Incentive Scheme	12,052	12,072
Advanced Access	4183	4233
Flu Immunisations	621	621
Clinical Workshop	–	240
Prescribing Incentive Scheme	–	228
	49,676	39,048

Chapter 9

How GPs get paid

General practitioners provide services *for* the National Health Service, as opposed to being given a contract *of* service, which is the case for hospital doctors. The difference between a 'contract *for* services' and a 'contract *of* services' means that the GP has Independent Contractor status which gives the GP the right to be self-employed and the right to manage their own affairs. The GP is responsible for employing staff, controlling the finances and is able to choose what services are provided to patients.

The new GMS contract (sometimes called 'the new contract') came into effect on 1 April 2004 and provides an unprecedented level of investment into primary care between 2003/04 and 2005/06 – raising total spend (by the government) by 33%.

The new contract is a practice-based contract which allows practices to control their workload by providing them with the ability to choose the services they will provide.

All GMS practices provide essential and additional services. They can provide enhanced services, if commissioned to do so by the Primary Care Organisation (PCO).

Essential services

Essential services cover the management of patients who are ill (or believe themselves to be ill) and the general management of patients who are terminally ill. It also covers the management of chronic disease (in the manner determined by the practice, in discussion with the patient).

Global sum

The global sum is the funding for practices to cover the cost of essential and additional primary care services.

The practice list is multiplied by the allocation formula to give a weighted list size. The allocation formula is intended to ensure that the money flows according to patient need rather than distribution of doctors.

Global sum allocation formula

The formula aims to allocate resources to practices based on workload and the unavoidable costs of delivering high quality care to the local population. The allocation formula is based on the following:

- an adjustment for the age and sex of the population of the practice
- an adjustment for the additional needs of the population, relating to morbidity and mortality
- an adjustment for list turnover
- a nursing and residential homes index
- an adjustment for the unavoidable costs of delivering services to the population including a Market Forces Factor and rurality index

The amount for the global sum is the weighted list multiplied by £54. If the practice is a London practice they will also receive a London weighting adjustment, which is calculated as the registered list multiplied by £2.18.

The PCO will also add to the global sum an amount for Temporary Patients Adjustment, superannuation premium and appraisal premium.

The global sum is recalculated quarterly for changes in list size and weighting and is paid monthly.

Minimum Income Protection Guarantee correction factor

The MIPG correction factor is essentially designed to protect a practice's income and to ensure all practices start from a neutral position. It is needed because 80% of practices would receive less income under the new GMS contract than they did under the old contract.

For those practices that need the MIPG correction factor, this will be an additional monthly payment on top of their global sum. The MIPG correction factor would have been calculated at 1 April 2004. The first step to this correction is to calculate the practice's income earned under the old Red Book which is now being funded through the global sum – this is known as the global sum equivalent (GSE). The MIPG correction factor is calculated by deducting the global sum at 1 April 2004 from the global sum equivalent.

In future the MIPG correction factor payments will only be uprated by the same percentage as the global sum amount per patient. For example, if it is decided that the £54 will increase by 2%, then the correction factor will also be uplifted by 2%.

Opt-outs of additional services

Practices have a preferential right to provide additional services, but they may opt out. Opt-outs can be temporary or permanent. The cost to opt out of any additional services is calculated as a percentage of the global sum as follows:

Cervical screening	– 1.1%
Contraceptive services	– 2.4%
Vaccinations and immunisations	– 2.0%
Childhood immunisations and pre-school booster	– 1.0%
Child health surveillance	– 0.7%
Maternity medical services	– 2.1%
Minor surgery	– 0.6%
Out of hours	– 6.0%

Quality and Outcomes Framework

Participation in the Quality and Outcomes Framework (QOF) is voluntary. It is designed to reward high quality care and management through participation in an annual quality improvement cycle.

Practices can significantly increase their income under the quality and outcomes framework.

The points for each domain for 2004/05 and 2005/06 were as follows:

Clinical (76 indicators)	550
Organisational (56 indicators)	184
Patient experience (4 indicators)	100
Additional services (10 indicators)	36
Holistic care	100
Quality	30
Improved access bonus	50
	1050

Each point was worth £77.50 in 2004/05 and £124 in 2005/06 for an average practice (i.e. a list of 5891 patients). Therefore, practices need to calculate what a point is worth to them by dividing their registered list by 5891 and multiplying by the amount per point.

The clinical points will also take account of the disease prevalence of the practice compared to the average. This will result in an adjustment to the value per point for clinical indicators.

Practices will also be paid a monthly aspiration payment. In 2004/05 the yearly **aspiration** payment was calculated as one-third of the points that the practice aspires to, divided by 12 to give the monthly aspiration payment. For example, if the average practice aspired to 900 points in 2004/05, then the total amount due would be £69,750 (900 x £77.50). The aspiration payment would be one-third (of £69,750), which is £23,250. The practice would then be paid in 12 monthly instalments giving an amount of £1937.50.

At 31 March 2005, the number of points the practice had actually achieved was recorded and then the practice received an **achievement** payment for the balance owed to them. In this example, if the practice achieved 950 points then the total amount earned would be £73,625 (950 x £77.50); they would already have received a total aspiration payment of £23,250, leaving a balance due of £50,375. (This example ignores the impact of the disease prevalence. Disease prevalence will affect the value per point for clinical points only, i.e. if a point is worth £77.50 for an average practice, then after disease prevalence it may only be worth £70.) This would have been paid in April or May 2005.

In 2005/06 the yearly aspiration payment is calculated as 60% of the practice's total income earned from the quality and outcomes framework in 2004/05, and again this will be paid in 12 monthly instalments. In this example, the practice earned £73,625. The aspiration payment in 2005/06 would be 60% of £73,625 giving £44,175. As the amount per quality point increases to £124 the aspiration payment would be adjusted to take account of the fact that the amount per point has increased. So the £44,175 will be multiplied by £124, divided by £77.50 to give £70,680. This would be paid in 12 instalments of £5890 per month.

Enhanced services

These are essential or additional services delivered to a higher standard or services not provided through essential or additional services.

Enhanced services are split between directed, national and local. Practices have to agree with their PCO which services they will be commissioned to provide.

Directed enhanced services

Improved access

The aspiration payment is £2580.50 x CPI. An aspiration payment is made up-front to ensure practices' commitment to deliver 48 hour access. A reward payment of £2580.50 x CPI (contractor population index) is received if the practice has achieved providing 48 hour access throughout the year.

Contractor Population Index

Funding under the new contract is based on an average practice with a list size of 5891 patients. Income in the SFE (Statement of Financial Entitlement) is given as an amount for the average practice, so to calculate income for a practice, one needs to multiply the amount for the average practice by the practice's CPI. The CPI is calculated by dividing the practice's registered list by 5891.

Childhood vaccinations

Amounts below are for an average list with 59.25 two-year olds and 61.45 five-year olds. To calculate actual payment, prices below are multiplied by the ratio of patients in these age bands to 59.25 and 61.45.

Age 2 years
lower target (70%)   £2740.62 per annum
higher target (90%)   £8221.87 per annum

Age 5 years
lower target (70%)   £848.51 per annum
higher target (90%)   £2544.50 per annum

For example, if the number of children aged 2 years on the practice list is 45 and they have reached the higher target, the payment calculation is as follows:

$45 / 59.25 \times 8221.87 = £6244.45$

This amount would be paid quarterly, therefore the amount for one-quarter would be £1561.11.

Flu and pneumococcal vaccinations

The payment is £7.28 per patient aged 65 or over.

Minor surgery

Fees depend on the complexity of the procedure; for example:
- joint injection   £41.29
- cutting surgery   £82.58

Supporting staff dealing with violent patients

The retainer per GP is £2064.50.

National enhanced services

National specifications and benchmark fees for providing these services have been developed. PCOs commissioning these services will need to consider local need using the specifications, but as a guide only. National enhanced services cover the following:
- anti-coagulant monitoring
- provision for near-patient testing
- specialist care of patients with depression
- care for patients who are alcohol misusers

- IUD fittings
- care for patients suffering from drug misuse
- more specialised services for patients with multiple sclerosis
- intra-partum care
- provision of immediate and first response care
- minor injury services
- enhanced care of homeless
- more specialised sexual health services

For the latest guidelines of fees, please refer to the Medeconomics UK database in *GP Magazine*.

Local enhanced services

Payments for local enhanced services will be subject to local negotiation.

Seniority

'Seniority' rewards GPs for their working commitment to the NHS. The amount a GP receives will depend upon the number of years of reckonable service within the NHS. The number of years service will be calculated since the date a GP first became registered with the NHS.

Seniority is also linked to the GP's superannuable earnings. If a GP receives more than the average superannuable earnings they will receive their full entitlement of seniority. If a GP's superannuable earnings are between one-third and two-thirds of the average, they will receive 60% of their entitlement. If below one-third, the GP will not receive any seniority.

Personal Medical Services Practices

The 1997 Primary Care Act introduced PMS Pilots. Essentially, the Act gave the practice the option to opt out of General Medical Services (GMS) and move away from the constraints of the Red Book. Instead, a PMS could negotiate it's own contract with the Health Authority for a range of services provided.

PMS providers are able to benefit from the same advantages as those agreed under the New GMS contract. PMS providers were originally on pilot schemes; however, from 1 April 2004 this became a permanent option.

PMS funding will continue to practices through previously agreed baselines. PMS practices can also participate in the quality and outcomes framework. However, there was a deduction of 168 quality points in 2004/05 and a deduction of 105 points for 2005/06 from the total achieved. The reason for this was that PMS practices should already have been providing a level of quality care. PMS practices can also discuss with their PCO what enhanced services they can be commissioned to provide.

Reimbursements

GPs are reimbursed for some of their expenses. The main reimbursements are shown below.

Rent and rates

GPs are eligible for rent and rates reimbursements. The scheme is designed to cover the cost of the GP providing accommodation, whether rented or owned by the GP.

If a GP rents the premises, and the PCO are satisfied with the level of accommodation provided, the PCO will reimburse fully the costs of rent, rates, water and refuse charges.

Under the old contract if the GP owned the premises, they would either be reimbursed on a cost rent basis or a notional rent basis. Under the new contract, practices in receipt of a cost rent or notional rent will continue to receive this, as long as there are no changes in circumstances.

Cost rent seeks to reimburse the interest charges on the cost of a new or modified surgery. It should be noted that the repayment of capital is up to the GP.

Notional rent is assessed every 3 years by the district valuer who determines the current market rent that might reasonably be expected to be paid for the premises.

GPs who also own their premises will also be fully reimbursed for rates, water rates and refuse rates.

Staff reimbursements

Under the old contract GPs were reimbursed 70% of the cost of their staff. Under the new contract this is now funded through the global sum. Therefore GPs will no longer get a direct reimbursement for their staff costs.

Other reimbursements

There are also reimbursements available for:
- cost of drugs
- locum allowance
- associate allowance
- golden hello
- returners scheme
- flexible careers scheme
- doctors retainer scheme

Chapter 10

Taxation and superannuation

Taxation

The Inland Revenue introduced self-assessment from the tax year 1996/97. Each taxpayer is required to complete a detailed tax return, which declares all their income. From this information the Inland Revenue calculates the individual's tax liability.

Each partnership is required to complete a partnership tax return, from which each partner takes their own profit share and includes it on their own tax return with details of income from other sources.

As the name suggests, the responsibility for completing and submitting the tax return to the Inland Revenue and paying the tax by the relevant deadlines lies with the individual.

Calculation of taxable profits

If you are a partner in a partnership, the way your taxable profits are calculated is more complicated, especially if the practice year end is not the same as the tax year end. The tax year runs from 6 April to 5 April the following year.

As a partner you are taxed on your share of profits, which will be shown on the profit allocation page, and not on the monthly drawings you have received. This is a common misunderstanding.

Practices do not necessarily prepare accounts to the same tax year. An individual is taxed on the profits of the accounting period ending in the current tax year. For example, accounts prepared to 31 March 2005 will be taxed in the year 2004/05 (6 April 2004 to 5 April 2005); accounts for the year ended 30 June 2004 will also be taxed in the year 2004/05 as this accounting year end falls into the tax year 2004/05.

The figure, which appears on the tax return as taxable profits, will never be the same as the figure per the profit allocation. The reason for this is that some items are not tax deductible and also personal expenses that are claimed will be deducted from the profits.

Capital allowances

Included in the accounts is an amount for depreciation of the assets. As mentioned in Chapter 5, the rate at which assets are depreciated depends on the assets themselves and the accountant. Depreciation is not an allowable expense for tax purposes, however, it is replaced by capital allowances.

The allowance given on the cost of assets is at 25% on the reduced balance brought forward (the balance brought forward will be the cost of the asset less the capital allowances deducted in previous years). Current tax law allows capital allowances on assets bought in their first year at 40%. For cars the maximum eligible cost is £12,000. If the cost is in excess of £12,000, the capital allowances for the year are restricted to £3000 until the value of the car is below £12,000.

Example of capital allowances, where FYA is first year allowance:

	Fixtures and fittings	Motor car
Year 1		
Cost	£24,000	£15,000
FYA @ 40%	(£9600)	
Capital allowance (restricted)		(£3000)
Written down value carried forward	£14,400	£12,000

Year 2
Capital allowances at 25%	(£3600) (25% of £14,400)	(£3000)
Written down value carried forward	£10,800 (£14,400−£3600)	£9000

Personal expenses

Self-employed GPs can claim their expenses, which are 'wholly and exclusively' incurred in the performance of their duties. The following expenses can be claimed for tax relief:
- motor expenses (business use only)
- professional subscriptions
- telephones (including mobiles) – business use only
- professional proportion of use of home
- personally bought drugs and instruments
- printing, postage and stationery
- medical books and journals
- professional laundry
- personal accountancy fees

However, for an employed GP, the expenses that can be claimed have to be 'wholly, exclusively and **necessarily**' incurred in the performance of their duties. The additional criteria of necessity makes a dramatic difference between the expenses a self-employed GP and an employed GP can claim. Employed GPs would only be able to claim the following:
- professional subscriptions
- business mileage using the Inland Revenue rates

How self-employed GPs pay their tax

Under self assessment, individuals pay tax at the end of January and July each year on their self-employed income. On each date a payment on account (a prepayment) for the next tax year is paid; this is usually half of the previous year's total tax liability (see example below). Once your tax return has been prepared you may have to make a balancing payment or be due a refund depending on whether your actual tax liability for the year is more or less than the payments you have already made. So if your income has gone up since the previous tax year, you will have a balance due in the following January together with the first payment on account for the following tax year.

Example of tax payments for 2004/05	
31 January 2005	
First payment on account 2004/05	£5000
31 July 2005	
Second payment on account 2004/05	£5000

Once the tax return has been completed the actual tax due will be compared with the payments on account and any difference will be paid in January 2006. For example, if the total tax due for 2004/05 was £20,000 the tax liability in January 2006 would be:

31 January 2006	
Balance 2004/05 (£20,000 - £5000 – £5000)	£10,000
First payment on account 2005/06 (half of the tax due 2004/05)	£10,000
Total tax payable	£20,000
31 July 2006	
Second payment on account 2005/06	£10,000

Example of tax payments

Dr Green is a partner in the Medical Centre, whose accounts are prepared to 30 June 2004. His tax return indicates that his total tax liability for 2004/05 is £34,000. He has already paid payments on account for 2004/05 in January 2005 and July 2005 of £14,000 each. His future tax liabilities are as follows:

31 January 2006
Balance for 2004/05   £6000 (£34,000 – £14,000 – £14,000)
First payment on
account 2005/06   £17,000 (£34,000 × 50%)
                              £23,000

31 July 2006
Second payment on
account 2005/06   £17,000 (£34,000 × 50%)

National Insurance

National insurance (NI) is paid towards the cost of an individual's state pension and benefits.

Self-employed GPs are required to pay both Class 2 and Class 4 NI. Class 2 is currently £2.10 per week which is usually collected by setting up a direct debit. Class 4 is calculated based on a GPs taxable profits; the amount for 2004/05 was calculated as 8% on profits from £4745 to £31,720, and a further 1% on profits above £32,720. Class 4 is calculated and paid with the tax liabilities on 31 January and 31 July.

Pensions

GPs have been included in the NHS Pension Scheme since it was established in 1948. GPs automatically become members, unless they decide not to join.

GPs contribute 6% of their pensionable income. In the past the PCO, as their notional employer, contributed the employer's amount, which since 1 April 2004 has been 14%. The global sum now includes the money to pay the employers contribution of 14%, so in effect GPs contribute 20% into the scheme, 6% is their contribution and 14% the employer's contribution.

Under the new GMS contract, a GP's superannuation contributions will be calculated based on their NHS profits. This is a major change to the scheme and replaces the old system where superannuation was calculated based on three classes of income. GPs are required to complete and sign a form detailing the calculation of their NHS profits.

Glossary

Assets
Assets are items that the practice own or amounts that are owed to them. For example, if they own the premises, this is an asset, and any money in the bank account is also an asset. The assets can be divided into 'fixed' and 'current' assets. Fixed assets represent long term assets (often the premises), whereas current assets represent short term assets such as cash.

Balance sheet
The profit and loss account shows the income and expenses for the accounting period, and usually covers a 12 month period. In contrast, the balance sheet shows the values of the assets and liabilities on a <u>single day</u>.

Capital and current accounts
The terms 'capital account' and 'current account' are generally interchangeable and refer to the wealth of the practice. The total of a partner's capital and current account is the amount of money they have invested in the practice and it will be this amount that they are entitled to when they leave.

Creditors and accruals
This is the amount owed to third parties at the year-end. For example, drugs purchased during the accounting period, but not paid for by the time of the year-end.

Current assets

Current assets are short-term assets which can be turned into cash within the next 12 months. These include stock of drugs, debtors and bank funds. The value of these will change from day to day. For example, the money in the bank account will change due to income being received and overheads being paid.

Debtors

Debtors comprise money that is owed from third parties to the practice. The practice will have completed this work within the accounting period but not yet received payment for it. For example, medical reports may have been written and sent to solicitors, but the income may not be received until after the year-end.

Depreciation

The reduction in the value of an asset due to wear and tear is measured by what is known as depreciation. Depreciation is a way of 'writing off' the cost of the asset over its useful economic life. Depreciation is shown as an expense in the profit and loss account each year.

Gross profit

For a trading business which buy goods at one price and then sells the same goods at a higher price, gross profits represent the difference between the two costs.

Liabilities

Liabilities are amounts that the practice owes. For example, the mortgage for the premises is a liability, as it is owed to the lender.

Net book value

The net book value is the original cost of the asset less the depreciation that has been charged to date. The net book value is an estimate of the value of the asset if sold at the accounting year end.

Net equity

This is the difference between the value of the premises and the balance outstanding on the mortgage. If a practice is in negative equity, it means that their mortgage is higher than the value of the premises.

Net profit
The net profit is the final profit that the business has made, after deducting all the expenses incurred (in running the business) from the income.

Overheads
Overheads are the expenses that are incurred in the day-to-day running of the practice, for example, salaries and wages of the practice staff.

Profit allocation
The partners in the practice are entitled to a share of profits; this is the net profit they have earned for the period. The profit allocation shows how the net profit for the period is shared amongst the partners.

Profit and loss
The profit and loss account (sometimes known as the income and expenditure account) shows the income, expenses and net profit for a given time period.

Profit sharing ratios
The profit sharing ratios (PSR) are the ratios in which a partnership shares the net profit.

Tangible assets
These will be the premises (if owned), fixtures, fittings, and office and medical equipment. The value of the premises on the balance sheet may be represented by either the original cost to purchase or build the property, or the open market value of the property. The open market value is the value that the practice would receive if they sold the premises.

Index

Minimum Income Protection Guarantee (MIPG), 43, 48–49
Mortgage, 11–13, 15, 20, 23, 31–32, 64

National Insurance, 61
Negative equity, 13
Net book value, 26, 28–29, 64
Net equity, 12–13, 31–32, 38, 64
Net profit, 3, 5, 8–10, 64
New contract, *see* 'The new contract'
Notes, 7, 9, 17, 38
Notional (rent), 19–20

Opt outs, 49
Overdrawn, 16, 34
Overheads, *see* Expenses

Payment on account, 59–60
Pension, 61
Personal Medical Services (PMS), 7, 47, 49, 53–54
Practice statistics, 41
Premises, 15–17, 32, 38, 54, 64
Prepayments, 14
Prior allocation, 19–21, 23, 39, 65
Profit, 2, 5, 22, 33–34
Profit and loss account, 1–3, 5, 6–7, 26, 37–38, 65
Profit sharing ratios (PSR), 19–22, 31, 35, 57, 65

Profitability, 2, 5, 8–9
Property, *see* Premises
Public Limited Company (PLC), 2

Quality and Outcome Framework, 43, 45, 49, 51

Red Book, 49
Reimbursements, 7, 20, 44, 54

Salaries, 7
Schedules, 7, 9, 38, 41–42
Seniority, 20, 23, 43, 53
Share of profits, *see* Profit sharing ratios
Statement of Financial Entitlement (SFE), 51
Superannuation, 33–35, 61

Tangible assets, 12, 15, 25, 29, 39, 65
Tax, 22, 33, 37, 57, 59–60
Tax return, 1, 5, 59
Tax year, 6, 58
'The new contract', 47, 49

Wages, 7
Wear and tear, 25
Writing off (written off), 25, 64

Year-end (date), 6, 12, 14, 63